Scientists Who Made History

Isaac NEWTON

Paul Mason

WAYLAND
www.waylandbooks.co.uk

Published in 2014 by Wayland

Produced for Wayland by White-Thomson Publishing Ltd
www.wtpub.co.uk
+44 (0)843 208 7460

Editor: Polly Goodman
Designer: Derek Lee
Picture Researcher: Shelley Noronha, Glass Onion Pictures
Cover and Title Page Illustrator: Richard Hook
Science Panel Illustrator: Derek Lee
Map Illustrator: Tim Mayer
Consultant: Dr Brian Bowers, Senior Research Fellow at the Science Museum, London.
Proofreader: Kay Barnham

First published in Great Britain in 2001 by Wayland

British Library Cataloguing in Publication Data
Mason, Paul
Isaac Newton. - (Scientists Who Made History)
1. Newton, Sir Isaac, 1642–1727
2. Physicists - Great Britain
3. Physicists - Great Britain
I. Title
530'.092

ISBN 978 0 7502 8477 6

Printed in China

10 9 8 7 6 5 4

Picture Acknowledgements: AKG 5b, 28, 36, 39; Bridgeman 5t, 9, 13, 18, 23, 30, 31, 37b, 38, 44b; Corbis 6, 7, 27, 42; Mary Evans 12, 16, 20, 24, 25, 33, 34, 35; Hodder Wayland Picture Library 4, 11b, 17, 18, 21, 22, 29, 41, 45t; Local Studies Collection, Lincoln Central Library, by courtesy of Lincolnshire County Council, Education & Cultural Services Directorate 10, 11t, 15b, 44t; National Portrait Gallery 15t; Ann Ronan 32, 37t, 40, 43; Stockmarket 26.

Wayland
Hachette Children's Books
338 Euston Road
London NW1 3BH

Wayland Australia
Level 17/207 Kent Street
Sydney
NSW 2000

Wayland is a division of Hachette Children's Books, an Hachette UK Company.
www.hachette.co.uk

Contents

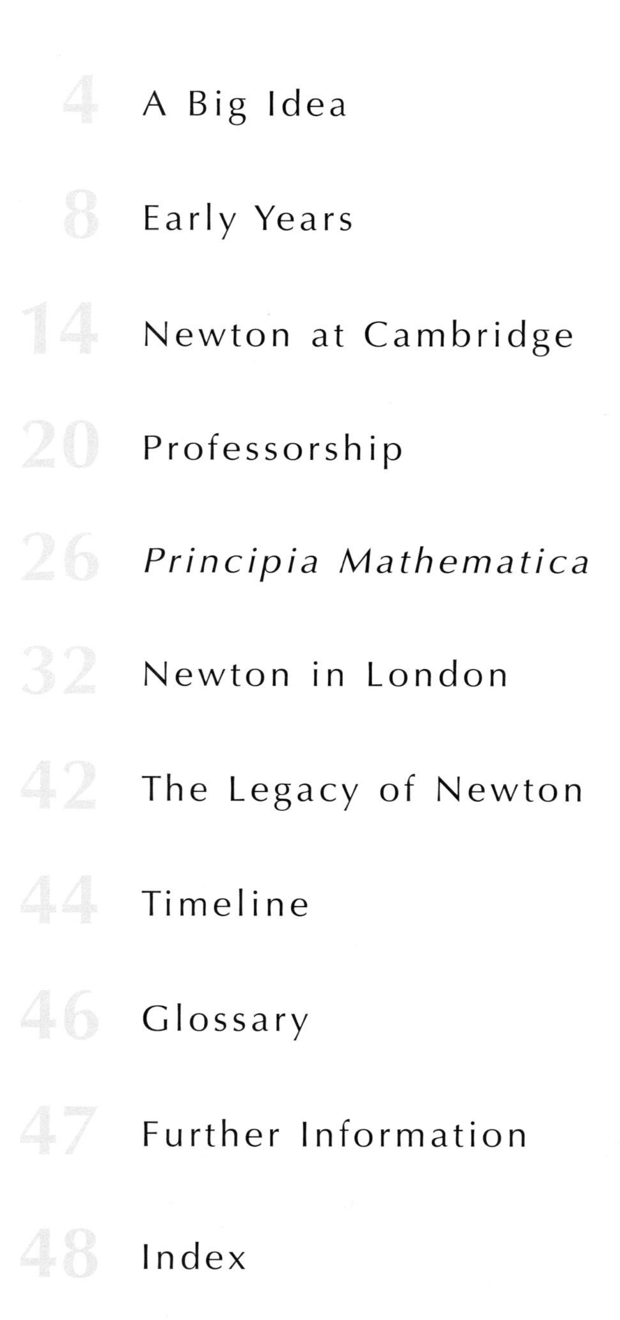

IN THEIR OWN WORDS

'I do not know what I may appear to the world, but to myself I seem to have been only like a boy playing on the sea-shore, and diverting myself in now and then finding a smoother pebble or a prettier shell than ordinary, whilst the great ocean of truth lay all undiscovered before me.'

ISAAC NEWTON, QUOTED IN *SPENCE'S ANECDOTES* (PUBLISHED IN 1820).

A Big Idea

THE YEAR WAS 1665, and all through London and in every large city in England, the plague was raging. Tens of thousands of people had already died of this mysterious disease, of which no one understood the cause. The university city of Cambridge had also been affected by the plague, and many academics were leaving for safer places in the countryside. Among them was a young man of about twenty-five years old, named Isaac Newton, who was headed for his family home at Woolsthorpe in Lincolnshire.

Back in Woolsthorpe, while sitting in a corner of an apple orchard, Newton was letting his mind wander when suddenly, right in front of him, an apple fell from the tree. The apple seemed to have an amazing effect on Newton. He wondered why the apple did not stay where it was, instead of falling towards the Earth.

Newton grabbed his notebook and started writing furiously, as if he had to get an idea down on paper before it left him. He thought that the apple's fall might help him explain how the universe was organized and he wanted to write down his ideas straight away.

BELOW: *This simple drawing shows citizens fleeing London in 1630 in an attempt to escape from an outbreak of the plague. But death, represented by the spear-wielding skeletons, seems to have accompanied them.*

ABOVE: *This portrait of Newton was painted in 1905. It shows the young scientist sitting in his family orchard in Woolsthorpe in 1665, with a book about the movement of planets in space.*

Who was Newton?

Isaac Newton, who died almost 300 years ago, was one of the greatest scientists ever to have lived. There are three main reasons for this:

- Newton was a brilliant mathematician – so brilliant that only a few people could understand his work.
- Newton wrote two books that changed the way people understood the world: one on how the universe works and one on light.
- Newton relied on proof. Today this sounds obvious, but when Newton was alive, scientists rarely tested their ideas thoroughly.

RIGHT: *This photo shows the actual orchard in which Newton sat. The apple tree is a descendant of the one that was there when he was alive.*

IN THEIR OWN WORDS

'Tis the truth of my experiments which is the business in hand. On this my Theory depends.'

ISAAC NEWTON WRITING ABOUT HIS SCIENTIFIC METHOD OF OBSERVATION AND EXPERIMENT, IN NOVEMBER 1676.

A NEW SCIENCE

Newton spent much of his time in Woolsthorpe working towards a mathematical proof of the force of gravity (the force that made the apple fall to the ground), although it was many years before he was finally able to produce this.

Science was at an exciting point during Newton's lifetime. Many breakthroughs were made, in chemistry, astronomy, mathematics and other sciences. But despite all the new discoveries, many scientists still worked in a very haphazard, unscientific way. Like the ancient Greek philosopher Aristotle, they often used clever arguments to explain how the world worked, and rarely tested their ideas using experiments.

RIGHT: *This is the title page of a book by Galileo Galilei, called* Dialogue Concerning the Two Chief Systems of the World. *Galileo, who died the year Newton was born, was called 'the founder of modern science' by Albert Einstein. Newton developed and proved some of Galileo's ideas.*

This was where Newton differed from almost all the others. He worked by trying to imagine an answer to a problem: for example, what keeps the planets in motion around the Sun. Then he conducted experiments to see if his imagined answer might be correct, and used mathematics to explain the experiments. This is the way in which scientists still work today.

IN THEIR OWN WORDS

'I would fain [like to] learn... the things that are, and understand their nature, and get knowledge of God.'

ISAAC NEWTON DESCRIBING HOW HE HOPED HIS ATTEMPTS TO UNDERSTAND HOW THE WORLD WORKED WOULD BRING HIM CLOSER TO GOD.

BELOW: *Galileo demonstrating his new, powerful telescope, with which he discovered stars and moons no one had ever seen before.*

IN THEIR OWN WORDS

'Sir Isaac Newton told me that when he was born he was so little they could put him in a quart pot... and so little likely to live that when two women were sent to North Witham for something for him, they sate [sat] down on a stile by the way and said there was no occasion for making haste as they were sure the child would be dead before they could get back.'

JOHN CONDUITT REMEMBERING A CONVERSATION WITH NEWTON IN AUGUST 1726.

Early Years

ISAAC NEWTON was born at 2 a.m. on Christmas Day, 1642, in the village of Woolsthorpe, Lincolnshire. His father, Robert, was a farmer, but he died three months before Isaac's birth. Isaac's house was called the 'manor house' by local people. Although it had only four rooms, it was far grander than the other villagers' homes.

When Isaac was born, he was so weak that he had to have a bolster round his neck to keep his head upright and his mother thought he would die. In the seventeenth century many children died as they were being born or soon afterwards. But Isaac survived, and he was baptized on 1 January 1643.

BELOW: *England in Newton's time. The smaller map shows England's position in the world.*

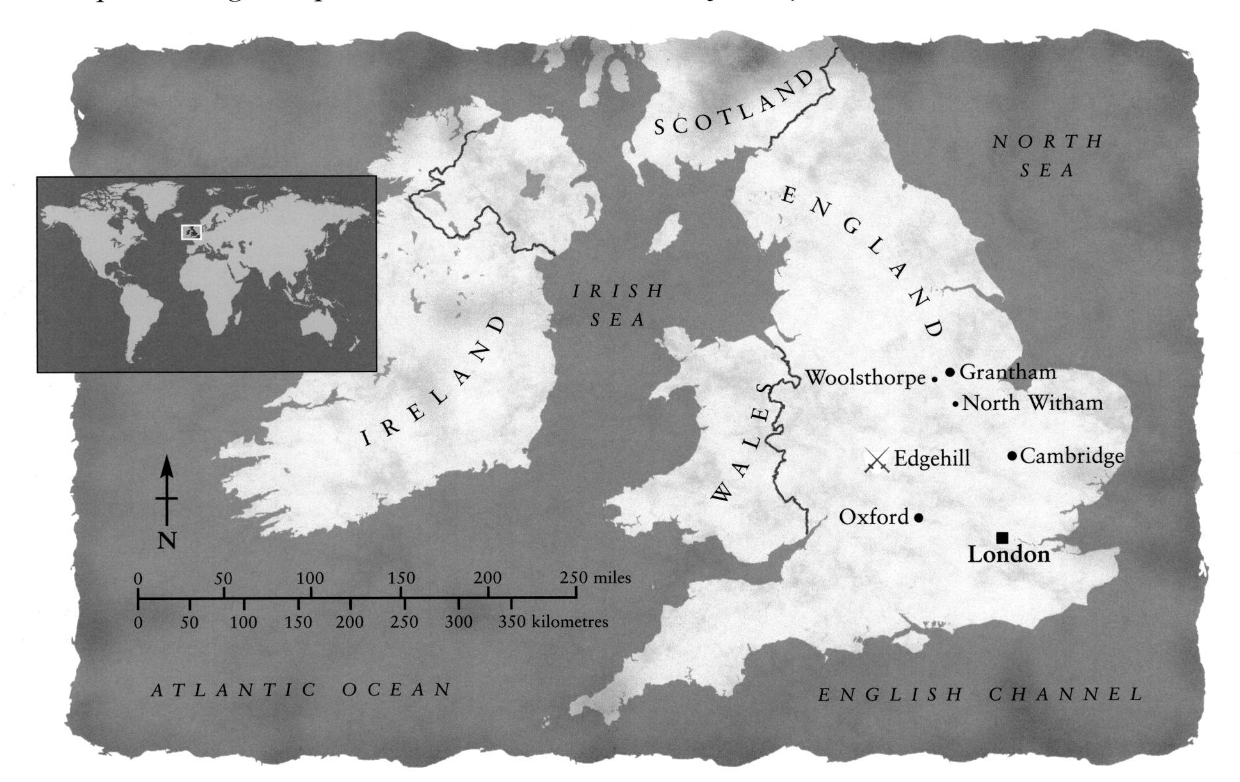

ABOVE: *This painting shows Isaac's family home, the 'manor house', where he spent most of his childhood living with his grandparents.*

Childhood

When Isaac was three years old, his mother, Hannah, remarried. Her new husband was the Reverend Barnabas Smith, who was the rector of a nearby church. Hannah was about thirty years old. Her new husband was sixty-three. The reason for their marriage is not certain, but it was probably a business arrangement. The Reverend was fairly wealthy and did not have very long to live. When he died, Hannah would inherit his wealth.

After the wedding, Isaac's mother went to live with the Reverend Smith in North Witham. She left Isaac behind in the manor house, where he was looked after by his grandparents. Isaac hated his mother's new husband, and bitterly resented the fact that she had left to live in North Witham. Although she came to visit, his mother did not return to live at the manor house for another eight years.

In 1653, the Reverend died and Hannah came back to Woolsthorpe, bringing with her three children (Mary, Benjamin and Hannah) from her second marriage. By this time Isaac was eleven years old. He had grown up without his mother there and it must have seemed very strange to have her back.

IN THEIR OWN WORDS

'[I remember] threatening my father and mother Smithe to burne them and the house over them.'

NEWTON REMEMBERS HIS HATRED OF HIS STEP-FATHER WHEN HE WAS A BOY, TAKEN FROM A NOTEBOOK WRITTEN LATER IN HIS LIFE.

ABOVE: *A painting of Newton aged twelve years old.*

SCHOOL DAYS

While his mother was away, Isaac went to the local primary school, where he learned to read and write. In 1655, it was decided that he should leave primary school and go to King's School in Grantham, the nearest large town. Grantham was seven miles away, which was too far to travel by pony or cart every day. So Isaac lodged with the family of a local apothecary (chemist).

King's School

During Isaac's first years at King's School, he studied Latin, Greek and the Bible. But he didn't do particularly well at his studies and he wasn't very popular. Since he had lived only with his grandparents for most of his life, he probably found it difficult to make friends with other children.

Isaac may not have been good at his studies, but he was good at model-making. At the age of about thirteen, Isaac discovered a book called *Mysteries of Nature and Art* by John Bate. It was full of instructions for making machines – windmills that turned, kites, sundials and paper lanterns. Isaac quickly read the book, completing all the models and then inventing machines of his own to make.

One day on his way to school, Isaac was kicked in the stomach by another pupil. He challenged the boy to a fight and won. Not satisfied by this victory, Isaac vowed that he would beat his opponent at school as well. Before long, he was near the top of the class, and the headmaster, Henry Stokes, was starting to think that he might be able to go to university.

ABOVE: *This picture shows the church-like inside of King's School in Grantham, where Isaac went for several years.*

RIGHT: *This is part of the windowsill at King's School in Grantham, where Isaac carved his name.*

The Apothecary's Shop

Isaac was fascinated by the work of the apothecary with whom he lodged, whose name was Clark. He begged to be allowed to watch Clark mix drugs and medicines in his shop, and soon began to note down the different ingredients that were used. Newton's fascination with illness later in life probably started when he saw so many sick people coming into the apothecary's shop for their medicines.

In 1658, Hannah took Isaac out of school. As the eldest son, he was expected to help run the farm. But sixteen-year-old Isaac had other ideas. He was so bad at his jobs on the farm (probably deliberately) that Hannah was finally persuaded to let him go back to school, to prepare for Cambridge University.

RIGHT: *The Battle of Edgehill took place on 23 October 1642, just two months before Newton was born. It was one of the great battles of the English Civil War. On the right is the Royalist Prince Rupert. On the left is a Parliamentarian soldier. Parliamentarians were called 'roundheads' because of the shape of their helmets.*

ABOVE: *The execution of King Charles I, in 1649. You can see some of the spectators rushing to dip their handkerchiefs in Charles's blood. The same thing happened more than 130 years later when the King of France was executed.*

Civil War

Newton's childhood was a turbulent time in England. Just before his birth, the English Civil War broke out between Royalists and Parliamentarians. The Royalists supported the right of King Charles I to rule the country. The Parliamentarians thought that Parliament should rule. Many of the Parliamentarians were also Puritans – people who rejected the elaborate religious worship of the official Church. The King and many of his supporters were Catholics – the very opposite of the Puritans.

In 1649, Charles I was beheaded and two years later, Charles II fled to France when Oliver Cromwell defeated his army. After Cromwell's death, Charles II returned to England in 1660 and was restored to the throne. The divisions the war had caused – especially the religious divisions – remained for many years afterwards.

IN THEIR OWN WORDS

'What a loss it was to the world, as well as a vain attempt, to bury so extraordinary a talent in the rustic business.'

ISAAC'S UNCLE OR A TEACHER, IN A LETTER PERSUADING HIS MOTHER TO SEND HIM TO UNIVERSITY.

Newton at Cambridge

ISAAC NEWTON arrived at Cambridge University in 1661. Cambridge then was a very different place from today. One visitor wrote to a friend that it was 'intolerably dirty... the buildings in many parts of town are so little and so low that they look more like huts for pygmies than houses for men.'

Even though his mother was relatively wealthy, Newton went there as a sizar – a student who paid for his studies by acting as a servant to his tutor and other more wealthy students. Sizars were regarded as outcasts by the other students, so Newton's first few years at Cambridge cannot have been an easy time.

BELOW: *A modern-day photo of Trinity College, at Cambridge University, which Newton first joined in 1661. In Newton's day, the students were not really supposed to mix with the people from the town. Instead, they were meant to lead a life of religious activity and study. This probably suited Newton very well.*

IN THEIR OWN WORDS

'[Newton] found [ancient Greek mathematics] so easy to understand that he wondered how anybody would amuse themselves to write any demonstrations of them.'

FRENCH MATHEMATICIAN ABRAHAM DEMOIVRE, DESCRIBING NEWTON'S VIEWS OF A BOOK BY EUCLID, AN ANCIENT GREEK MATHEMATICIAN, IN 1727.

LEFT: *René Descartes, the French philosopher and scientist who was at the cutting edge of scientific thought when Newton was at university. Although many of Descartes' ideas were subsequently found to be wrong, they helped people like Newton come up with theories that proved to be correct.*

BELOW: *A portrait of the young Newton at about the time he was an undergraduate at Cambridge.*

The courses at Cambridge were based largely on the teachings of the ancient Greek philosopher Aristotle. According to Aristotle, everything in the world was made up of four elements: earth, air, fire and water. Different substances, such as gold and lead, contained varying amounts of these elements. Aristotle rarely bothered to prove his ideas through experiment, which meant that in Newton's time he was starting to look decidedly old-fashioned.

However, new ideas were starting to arrive at Cambridge. Among them were the theories of the French philosopher René Descartes. One of the big questions of the day was about light. Descartes suggested, incorrectly, that light was caused by pressure on an 'ether' that linked all things together. Theories about light were at the cutting edge of scientific thinking, and they soon began to interest Newton.

RIGHT: *Newton and his laboratory assistant use a prism to split white light into its different colours.*

IN THEIR OWN WORDS

'I procured me a Triangular glass-prism, to try therewith the celebrated Phaenomena of Colours... having darkened my chamber, and made a small hole in my window-shuts, to let in a convenient quality of the sun's light, I placed my Prism at its entrance, that it might be refracted to the opposite wall. It was at first a very pleasing divertisement, to view the vivid and intense colours produced thereby; but after a while applying myself to consider them more circumspectly, I became very surprised...'

FROM NEWTON'S PAPER 'AN HYPOTHESIS EXPLAINING THE PROPERTIES OF LIGHT', DESCRIBING HIS EXPERIMENT WITH A PRISM.

LIGHT AND PLANETARY MOTION

When Newton arrived at Cambridge in 1661 he had only the most basic knowledge of mathematics. Within two years he was tackling some of the most complicated mathematical questions of the day.

Newton spent much of his time working on theories about light. In August 1664, he bought a prism at a local fair to use in his experiments. The prism helped him make important discoveries about the nature of light (see page 17). Like many scientists he took great risks with his health. He once looked directly at the Sun and had to spend three days in a darkened room before he could see again. Another time he put pressure on his eyeball with the point of a small knife, to find out what effect it would have on his vision.

Newton's discoveries about light were groundbreaking, but he was unwilling to publish them and make them public.

Throughout his life, Newton had to be pushed into publishing his work. His ideas on light weren't printed in full until his book *Opticks* appeared in 1704, forty years after he started work on it.

Planetary Motion

Newton also became interested in the movement of the planets while he was at Cambridge. The leading mathematicians of the day were exploring the mathematical properties of curves, to help them describe the movement of the planets around the Sun. Newton's next challenge was to try and solve this puzzle.

In 1665, even though he hadn't followed the official courses properly, Newton was awarded a degree by Cambridge University. He was now a graduate.

BELOW: *An illustration of Newton's prism experiment, from a book containing his memoirs and details about his work.*

THE COLOURS OF WHITE LIGHT

Newton's experiments with a prism helped him realize that white light was made up of different colours. Prisms could be used to break it up. Newton also realized that colours are the result of different objects reflecting different kinds of light. All the other colours are absorbed by them. An object that looks white reflects all light, while an object that looks black absorbs all light.

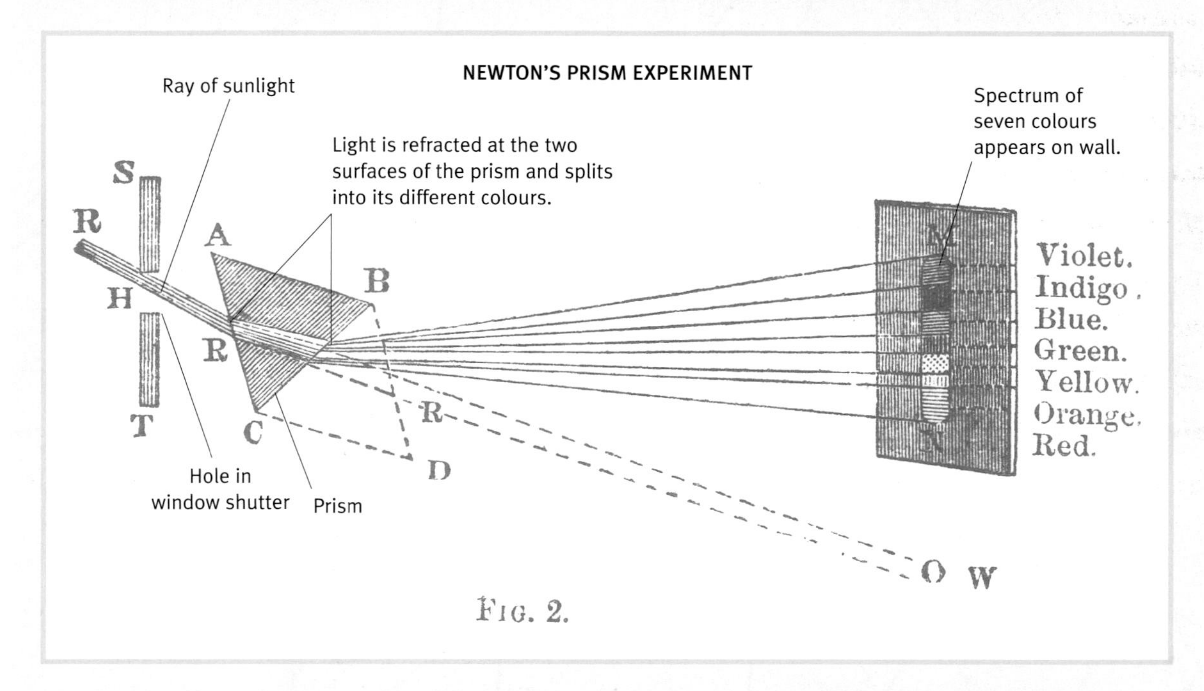

IN THEIR OWN WORDS

'In those days I was in the prime of my age for invention and minded Mathematicks and Philosophy more than at any time since.'

NEWTON REMEMBERS THE PLAGUE YEARS OF 1665–6 IN A PRIVATE LETTER.

THE PLAGUE YEARS

In 1665, the bubonic plague gripped England. The 'Black Death', as the plague was called, had appeared throughout the world at various times over the previous few hundred years. During its worst episode, from 1346 to 1349, about 25 million people were killed by the plague in Europe, North Africa and the Middle East: one person in every three.

The outbreak of 1665 was serious in England. The authorities declared quarantines for most major towns and discouraged people from travelling, to stop the spread of the plague. Newton left the 'intolerably dirty' town of Cambridge and returned to his family home in Woolsthorpe for almost two years. There he devoted his time to the problem of how to describe the circular motion of an object using mathematics. He hoped that this would help him understand about the movement of the Moon and the planets.

BELOW: *An early diagram from the 1600s showing the movements of the planets, all of which are travelling around the Sun in the centre of the illustration.*

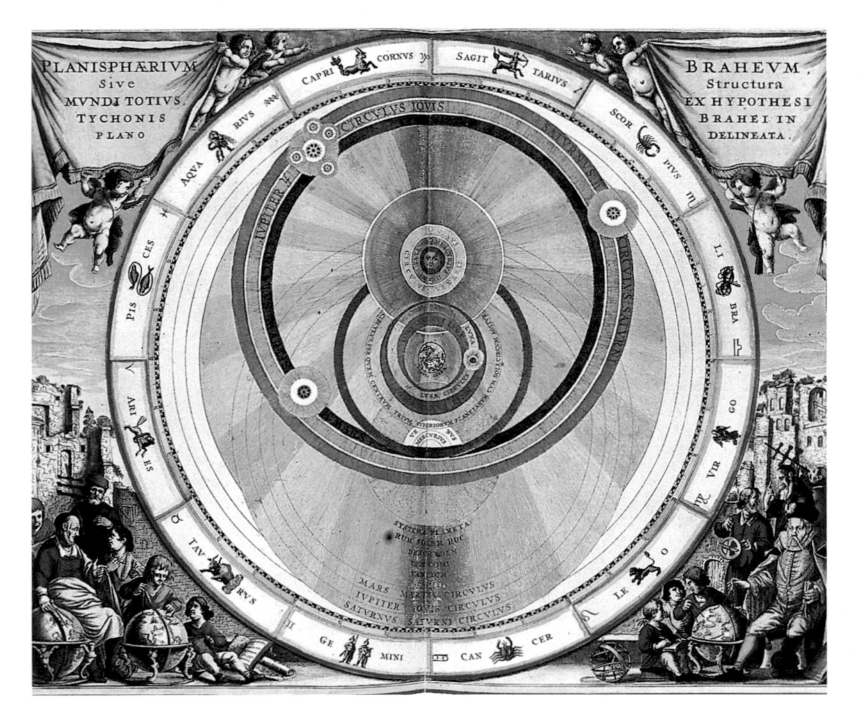

Calculus

While at Woolsthorpe, Newton also developed a mathematical method called calculus, which allowed him to work out the force with which a moving object pulls away from the centre of a circle. Newton used his new method to produce mathematical proof that there was a relationship between the force exerted by an object in circular motion and its distance from the centre of the circle (see the diagram on the opposite page for a demonstration of the inverse square law).

INVERSE SQUARE LAW

The illustration below shows how the inverse square law applies to planets travelling around the Sun. Planet A is 1 unit of distance from the centre of the Sun and exerts 1 unit of force. Planet B, which is 2 units of distance away from the centre of the Sun exerts only one-quarter of a unit of force. Planet C, which is 3 units of distance away, exerts one-ninth of a unit of force.

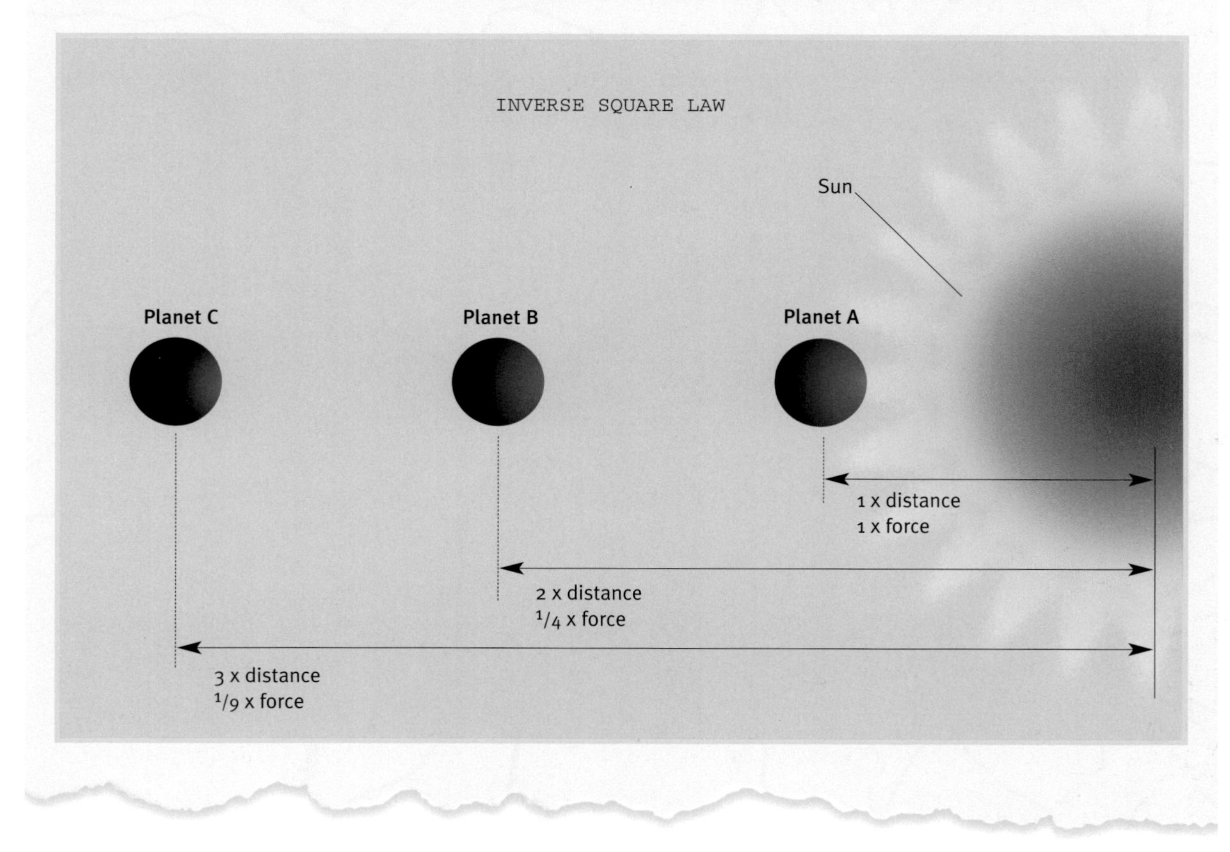

When Newton tried to apply the inverse square law to the movement of the Moon around the Earth it didn't work, so he abandoned the study. He didn't know that his law was right, but he was using the wrong radius of the Earth. The radius was 400 miles short. Since the distance from the centre of the Earth to the Moon was incorrect, this made the whole calculation wrong. An accurate figure for the Earth's radius only became available twenty years later, in 1685, at which time Newton was finally able to prove the inverse square law.

Professorship

BY MARCH 1667, the plague had died down and Newton returned to Cambridge to be made a Fellow. His academic future was now safe. As a Fellow, he was paid a small amount of money to continue his studies and teach. Newton's cleverness brought him to the attention of Isaac Barrow, who was a professor of mathematics at Cambridge. Newton began working as Barrow's assistant.

LEFT: *Isaac Barrow (1630–77), who was Professor of Mathematics at Cambridge University. Newton worked as Barrow's assistant for several years.*

In the autumn of 1669, just as the leaves on the Cambridgeshire trees were falling, Barrow resigned to take a better job in London. Newton, who Barrow recognized as a brilliant mathematician, replaced him. By this time Newton had been at Cambridge for eight years and was just 26 years old, but now he was a professor of mathematics.

Newton and Religion

Newton believed that God had set him a personal puzzle to solve by making the way in which the planets moved so difficult to understand. Newton certainly thought that by working out how the universe moved he would get a closer knowledge of God. This religious side of Newton's nature helped him to solve some of the great scientific problems. In Newton's religious world, where God was invisible but influenced every part of people's lives, the idea of something invisible affecting how things worked was believable.

BELOW: *Newton was a skilled and careful craftsman as well as a great mathematician, and he made one of the first-ever reflecting telescopes. This photo shows a replica, or copy, of Newton's telescope.*

IN THEIR OWN WORDS

'There is no way, without revelation, to come to the knowledge of [God] but by the frame of nature.'

NEWTON EXPLAINING WHY HIS ATTEMPTS TO UNDERSTAND HOW THE NATURAL WORLD WORKED WERE BRINGING HIM CLOSER TO GOD.

ARIANISM AND ALCHEMY

Newton was now a famous man, at least among other mathematicians, and by any measure he was a great success. He came from an ordinary country background, but had become the most senior professor of mathematics in the country. But he was secretly walking a tightrope, with ruin at his feet. Firstly, he was an Arian – a follower of a secret, forbidden religion that rejected the idea of the Holy Trinity. Newton's other dangerous secret was that he practised alchemy.

Alchemy was an ancient practice even in Newton's day, but it had been banned in England since 1404. Alchemists thought that they could change substances into other things. Most famously, they thought they could turn ordinary metals into gold, by changing the balance of Aristotle's four elements (see page 15) in a substance. Since alchemy was banned in England, alchemists hid the meaning of their writings in a secret language that could only be interpreted by another alchemist. This must have appealed to Newton, who didn't like to make his ideas easy to understand.

OBSERVATIONS

UPON THE

PROPHECIES

OF

DANIEL,

AND THE

APOCALYPSE

OF

St. *JOHN.*

In TWO PARTS.

By Sir *ISAAC NEWTON.*

LONDON,

Printed by J. DARBY and T. BROWNE in *Bartholomew-Cloſe.*

And Sold by J. ROBERTS in *Warwick-lane,* J. TONSON in the *Strand,* W. INNYS and R. MANBY at the Weſt End of St. *Paul's Church-Yard,* J. OSBORN and T. LONGMAN in *Pater-Noſter-Row,* J. NOON near *Mercers Chapel* in *Cheapſide,* T. HATCHETT at the *Royal Exchange,* S. HARDING in St. *Martin's lane,* J. STAGG in *Weſtminſter-Hall,* J. PARKER in *Pall-mall,* and J. BRINDLEY in *New Bond-ſtreet.*

M,DCC,XXXIII.

RIGHT: *The title page of one of Newton's religious books. Newton was fascinated with the history of ancient Christianity, and when he died there were more books on this subject in his library than on science.*

Newton may have been attracted to alchemy because it was based on using experiments to build up a personal store of knowledge about how things worked. This approach was central to Newton's scientific thinking. Alchemy was also based on the principle that the alchemist had to be pure and religious to be successful. This would certainly have appealed to Newton's religious side.

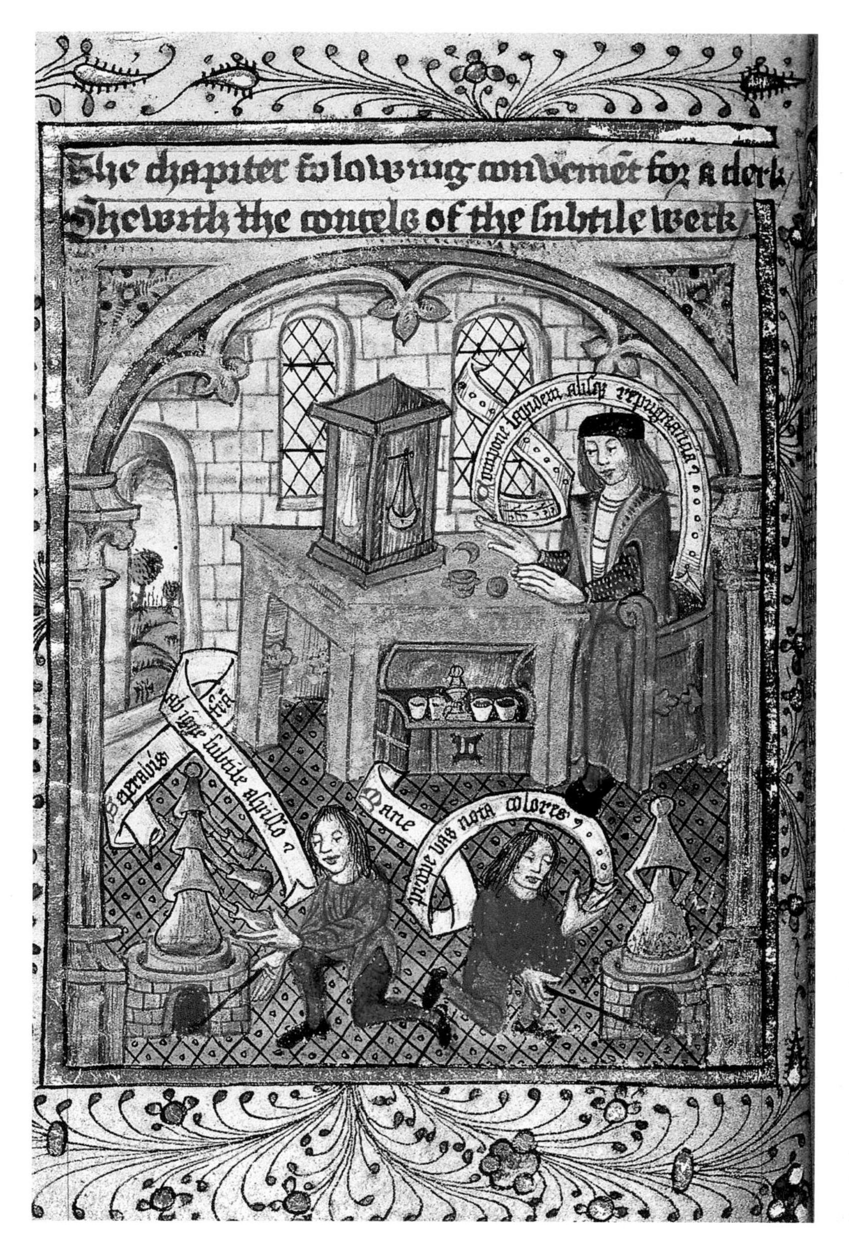

LEFT: *This painting from the 1400s shows an alchemist and his assistants preparing his materials. In fact, most alchemists worked alone and in secret, for fear that their ideas would be stolen or they would be discovered by the authorities.*

ALCHEMY

Alchemists aimed to produce a substance that could turn ordinary metal into gold. They called this substance the 'Philosopher's Stone'. The instructions below describe one recipe for making the substance.

1. Mix iron ore, mercury and acid.
2. Heat slowly for 10 days.
3. Dissolve what is left in acid under polarized light (from the Moon or a mirror).
4. Evaporate the liquid until it is solid again (this can take ten years or more).
5. Add potassium nitrate (gunpowder).
6. Seal in a special container and warm.

Rivalry with Hooke

In 1662, the Royal Society for the Promotion of Natural Knowledge had been formed in London. Many British scientists gathered there to discuss new ideas. The Society published papers and books, and conducted public experiments to demonstrate new theories. The man who arranged the demonstrations for the Society was a scientist named Robert Hooke.

In 1675, Newton was finally persuaded by the Secretary of the Society, Henry Oldenburg, to publish some of his ideas about light in a paper entitled 'An Hypothesis Explaining the Properties of Light'. Hooke immediately claimed that some of the ideas in the paper were based on his own work. The argument became a bitter dispute.

RIGHT: *The English astronomer Edmond Halley (1656-1742), who persuaded Newton to publish his proof of the inverse square law. Halley became famous for his work on comets. He calculated the orbit of a comet that he had seen in 1682 and predicted that it would return in 1758, which it did on Christmas Day of that year. This comet became known as Halley's Comet.*

Newton had made a powerful enemy in the Royal Society. Hooke became more powerful still when Henry Oldenburg and Isaac Barrow, each an important friend of Newton, died in 1677. Hooke became Secretary of the Royal Society, and Newton was isolated in the scientific world, with no friends and few supporters. He lapsed into silence and was scarcely heard of for seven years.

The Coffee-Shop Bet

One day in 1684, Robert Hooke, the astronomer Edmond Halley and the architect Sir Christopher Wren were arguing together in a coffee shop. The subject was whether there could be a mathematical proof for the inverse square law (see page 19). In an effort to win a bet he had made on the subject with the other men, Halley travelled to Newton's rooms in Cambridge, to talk to the great mathematician. After months of wrangling, Newton was finally persuaded to release his proof in a paper called 'On The Motion Of Moving Bodies'. It was this work that was to lead to one of his two masterpieces: the *Principia Mathematica*.

RIGHT: *The architect Sir Christopher Wren shows King Charles II his plans for rebuilding London after the Great Fire. Wren was also one of the people who made a bet that the inverse square law would be proved.*

Principia Mathematica

ALTHOUGH NEWTON'S DISPUTE with Robert Hooke started with his ideas on light, the argument went on to include 'On the Motion of Moving Bodies'. Newton became obsessed with finding and publishing a solution to the question of how the planets moved through space, partly so that he could finally prove Hooke wrong.

There were four key stages to Newton's work. Firstly, he established a mathematical proof of elliptical motion, rather than the circular motion he had proved in 'Moving Bodies'. This was important because planets were known to move in ellipses rather than perfect circles. Secondly, he proved that the comets that appeared in the skies of Europe during 1680 and 1682 were subject to the inverse square law.

LEFT: *A comet shoots across the night sky. The visit of a series of comets in the 1680s helped Newton in his work on planetary movement.*

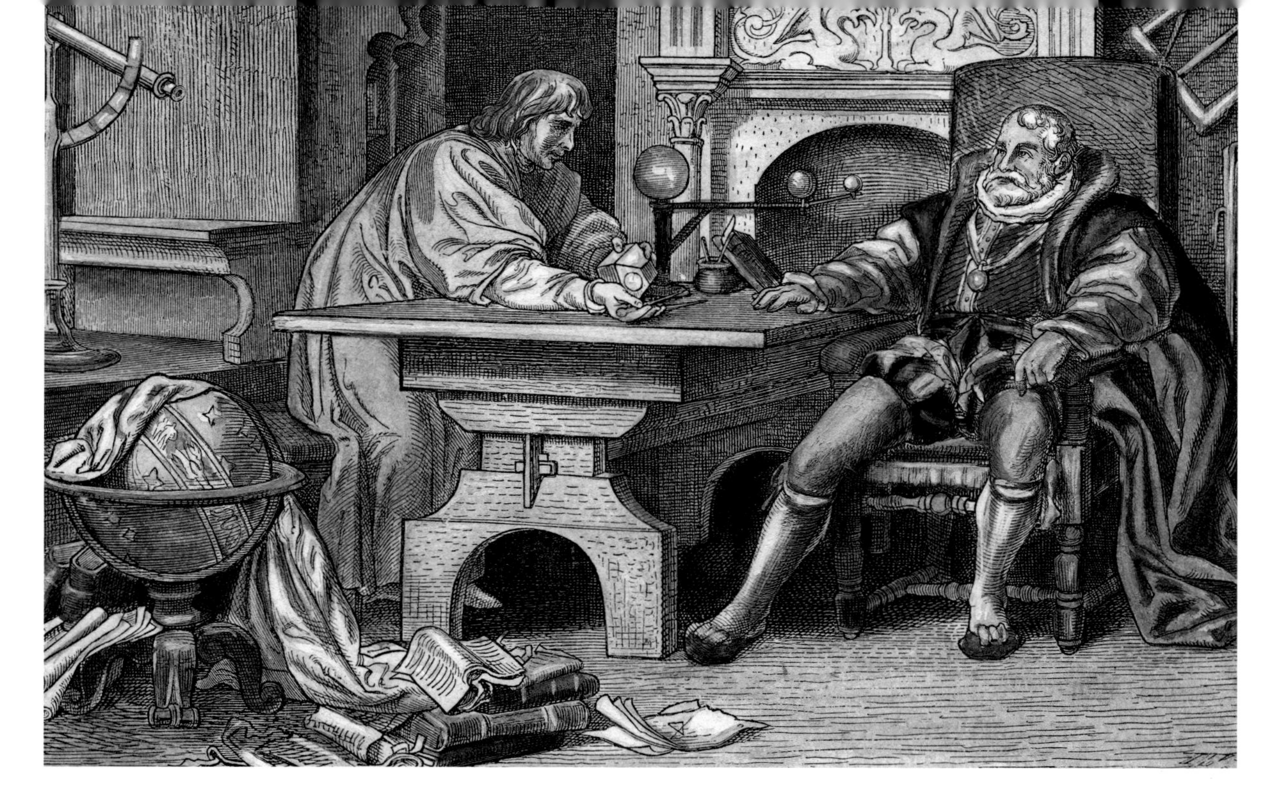

Thirdly, Newton began to think that gravity might operate across a distance and without a physical link. Finally, he used his method of calculus to prove a discovery by the astronomer Johannes Kepler, who said that planets travel fastest in their orbits when they are closest to the Sun.

Newton's new work was read out to a meeting of the Royal Society in December 1684. It was called 'On the Motion of Revolving Bodies', and though no one in the room could follow Newton's mathematical proofs, they realized that he was close to explaining how the planets moved through space. But Newton wasn't finished. He wanted to publish his ideas in full, so he spent the next year locked in his rooms in Cambridge, working on a full-length book.

ABOVE: *Johannes Kepler (left), whose work helped Newton develop his theories, explains his ideas to his patron, King Rudolph II (seated). Between them is a model of the Earth and Moon moving around the Sun.*

IN THEIR OWN WORDS

'The way therefore to examine it is by considering whether the experiments which I propound [put forward] do prove those parts of the theory to which they are applyed, or by prosecuting [doing] other experiments which the Theory may suggest for its examination.'

NEWTON EXPLAINS THE IMPORTANCE OF EXPERIMENTS, IN A LETTER OF 1672.

IN THEIR OWN WORDS

'He ate very sparingly, nay, sometimes he forgot to eat at all, so that going into his chamber I have found his [food] untouched... I never saw him take any recreation or pastime, either in riding out to take the air, walking, bowling or any other exercise whatever. Thinking all hours lost that were not spent in his studies, to which he kept so close that he seldom left the chamber...'

NEWTON'S ASSISTANT, HUMPHREY, REMEMBERING HOW HARD NEWTON WORKED.

Locked away

After the reading of 'On the Motion of Revolving Bodies', in December 1684, Newton hardly left his rooms. He worked constantly, snatching four or five hours of sleep a night and only eating when reminded to by his assistant.

Newton worked on through the winter of 1685–86. As the weather was getting warmer during the spring of 1686, Newton's first great work was almost finished. The book was called *Philosophiae Naturalis Principia Mathematica*, which is Latin for 'Mathematical Principles of Natural Philosophy'. It was arranged into four sections. An introduction explained what was to come; Books I and II explained Newton's work on forces and motion; and Book III applied the theories of Books I and II to actual situations. It was Book III that contained Newton's Theory of Universal Gravitation.

PHILOSOPHIÆ
NATURALIS
PRINCIPIA
MATHEMATICA.

AUCTORE
ISAACO NEWTONO, Eq. Aur.

Editio tertia aucta & emendata.

LONDINI:
Apud Guil. & Joh. Innys, Regiæ Societatis typographos.
MDCCXXVI.

RIGHT: *The title page of an edition of Newton's first great work, the* Principia Mathematica. *On the left-hand page is a portrait of the great scientist.*

Published

Principia was finally published by the Royal Society in the summer of 1687. In it, Newton explained how the universe worked: why the planets were in orbit, what caused the tides, and how comets travelled through space.

Newton had deliberately cloaked his ideas in language that was hard to understand: he didn't want to have to answer questions from anyone who couldn't understand what he was saying in full. His mathematical workings were also impossible to follow for all but a very tiny number of mathematicians. Even so, the book slowly got good reviews in academic journals across Europe. Today, it has been translated into many different languages throughout the world and has been published in over 100 editions in English.

IN THEIR OWN WORDS

'Having seen and read your book I think myself obliged to give you my most hearty thanks for having been at pains to teach the world that which I never expected any man should have known.'

DAVID GREGORY, PROFESSOR OF MATHEMATICS AT EDINBURGH UNIVERSITY, WRITES TO NEWTON AFTER THE PUBLICATION OF *PRINCIPIA MATHEMATICA*.

NEWTON'S LAWS OF MOTION

Law I

Every body stays motionless, or continues moving in a straight line, unless a force acts on it.

Law II

Any change in the movement of a body is always proportional to the force that acts on it, and is made in the direction of the straight line in which the force acts.

Law III

Every action has an opposite and equal reaction.

BELOW: *A cartoonist's view of Newton demonstrates the theory for which he was most famous: the theory of universal gravitation.*

NEWTON THE POLITICIAN

While Newton had been working on *Principia*, great changes had been taking place in England. In 1685, King Charles II had died and James II became king. James II was a Scotsman and a Catholic. To most people in England at this time, and certainly to Newton, the idea of a Catholic king was dreadful.

Neither Oxford nor Cambridge universities allowed Catholics to study there. When James II tried to force Cambridge to allow a Catholic priest to join the university, the professors protested. In 1687, Newton became an advisor in the battle to keep the priest out. It was his first taste of public affairs.

ABOVE: *This painting shows King James II being told that his rival William of Orange has landed in England. Within a short time, James had fled and William was crowned king.*

RIGHT: *John Locke (1632–1704), the philosopher who became one of Newton's closest friends.*

The university eventually lost the fight with James II, but before the priest could finish his studies, things had changed again. In 1688, James II was forced into exile by a new king, William of Orange, who was a Protestant. Parliament was called to oversee William's coming to power, and Newton, who had become known for his fight against Catholic influence, was elected a Member of Parliament.

Newton's position as a Member of Parliament lasted for just over a year. In London, he met Charles Mordaunt and Charles Montagu, both important politicians, and the philosopher John Locke. Locke's philosophy was based on the idea that all knowledge was based on experience, which echoed Newton's scientific approach, and Locke, like Newton, was strongly anti-Catholic. The two men became good friends.

IN THEIR OWN WORDS

'It is worth £500 or £600 a year, and has not too much business to require more attendance than you can spare.'

CHARLES MONTAGU EXPLAINS TO NEWTON THAT HIS DUTIES AS WARDEN MAY NOT BE VERY DEMANDING. IN FACT, NEWTON TOOK HIS DUTIES SO SERIOUSLY THAT HE OFTEN ARRIVED AT THE MINT AT 4.00 A.M.!

Warden of the Mint

In 1694 the Whigs, the political party to which many of Newton's friends belonged, came to power. Charles Montagu became Chancellor of the Exchequer, one of the most powerful jobs in the government, and in 1696 he offered Newton the job of Warden of the Royal Mint. Newton accepted, and on 26 April he boarded a horse-drawn coach at the Rose Inn in Cambridge and left the university for the last time. He was journeying to a new life in London.

Newton in London

NEWTON'S JOB AS Warden was to oversee the country's money supply. The Mint made new coins, and was responsible for the condition of coins in circulation. When Newton became Warden, some of Britain's coins were over 150 years old, and had very simple designs. They were easy to copy, and easier still to 'clip'. 'Clipping' was the art of removing a little gold or silver from the edge of a coin, then reshaping it to look normal. By 1696 workers were often paid in clipped coins that they could not use, and there were regular riots as a result.

On the edges of London were the 'liberties'. These were lawless places, where the poorest people lived and the police hardly dared to go. It was here that many clippers worked, and Newton and his officers pursued them, making arrests and sending criminals for punishment. Newton threw himself into the work with great energy, and was so successful that he received a number of death threats from clippers.

BELOW: *New coins being minted in 1750. Since the process was time-consuming, it took a long time for new coins to replace old ones. In Newton's day, some coins were over 150 years old!*

LEFT: *Prisoners in Newgate prison in 1735. Between June 1698 and Christmas 1699, Newton interviewed over 200 'clipper' witnesses, informers and suspects. During one week in February 1699, he had ten prisoners awaiting hanging in Newgate Prison.*

Recoinage

Newton also oversaw the recoinage of the whole country. Recoinage meant that all the old coins had to be brought back to the Mint, melted down, and turned into new coins that would be harder to copy or clip. Even so, Newton didn't abandon his mathematical skills. In January 1697, two mathematicians called von Leibnitz and Bernouili set a mathematical challenge which no one could solve. Details of the challenge reached Newton when he got home at 4.00 p.m. one afternoon. He sat down with a pencil and paper and, twelve hours later, the problem was solved.

IN THEIR OWN WORDS

'This vilifying of my Agents and Witnesses is a reflexion upon me which has gravelled [annoyed] me and must in time impair and perhaps wear out and ruin my credit.'

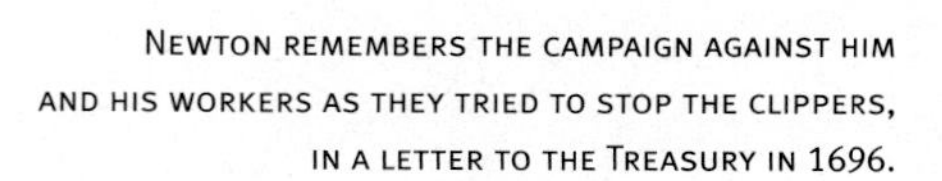

NEWTON REMEMBERS THE CAMPAIGN AGAINST HIM AND HIS WORKERS AS THEY TRIED TO STOP THE CLIPPERS, IN A LETTER TO THE TREASURY IN 1696.

CATHERINE BARTON

Newton's unofficial housekeeper in his London house was his niece, Catherine Barton. Newton also employed six servants. Catherine organized the house for him, arranging meals and parties, and overseeing the work of the servants. She was a clever, funny and lively woman, and she and Newton became close friends.

Catherine was also very beautiful. Many stories were told of men who fell in love with her the moment they saw her. One of these was the Chancellor of the Exchequer, Newton's friend Charles Montagu. He and Catherine probably lived together in secret until Montagu's death in 1715, although she was often back in Newton's house as a cover for their relationship. Within two years of Montagu's death, Catherine had married John Conduitt, who later wrote the first-ever biography of Newton.

RIGHT: *One of the houses in which Newton lived while in London, on the corner of St Martin's Street and Leicester Square.*

LEFT: *Charles Montagu, who later became an earl, was one of Newton's friends in London. He also had a close relationship with Newton's niece, Catherine Barton.*

Master of the Mint

In 1699 the old Master of the Mint died and Newton replaced him as head of the organization. He became involved in politics again in 1701, when he was elected a Member of Parliament, but rapidly backed out of public life. William of Orange died in 1702 and was succeeded by Queen Anne, who favoured the Tory party rather than Newton's Whigs.

In 1703, Newton focused his energy on a new role. That year, his old enemy Robert Hooke died and Newton was elected President of the Royal Society. He immediately began work on modernizing the Society, and on his next great book: *Opticks*.

IN THEIR OWN WORDS

'I had your two letters and am glad the air agrees with you, and though the fever is loath to leave you yet I hope it abates, and that the remains of the smallpox are dropping off apace... Pray let me know next how your face is and if your fever is going.'

NEWTON'S LETTER TO HIS NIECE CATHERINE BARTON, WHO WAS RECOVERING FROM SMALLPOX IN THE COUNTRYSIDE.

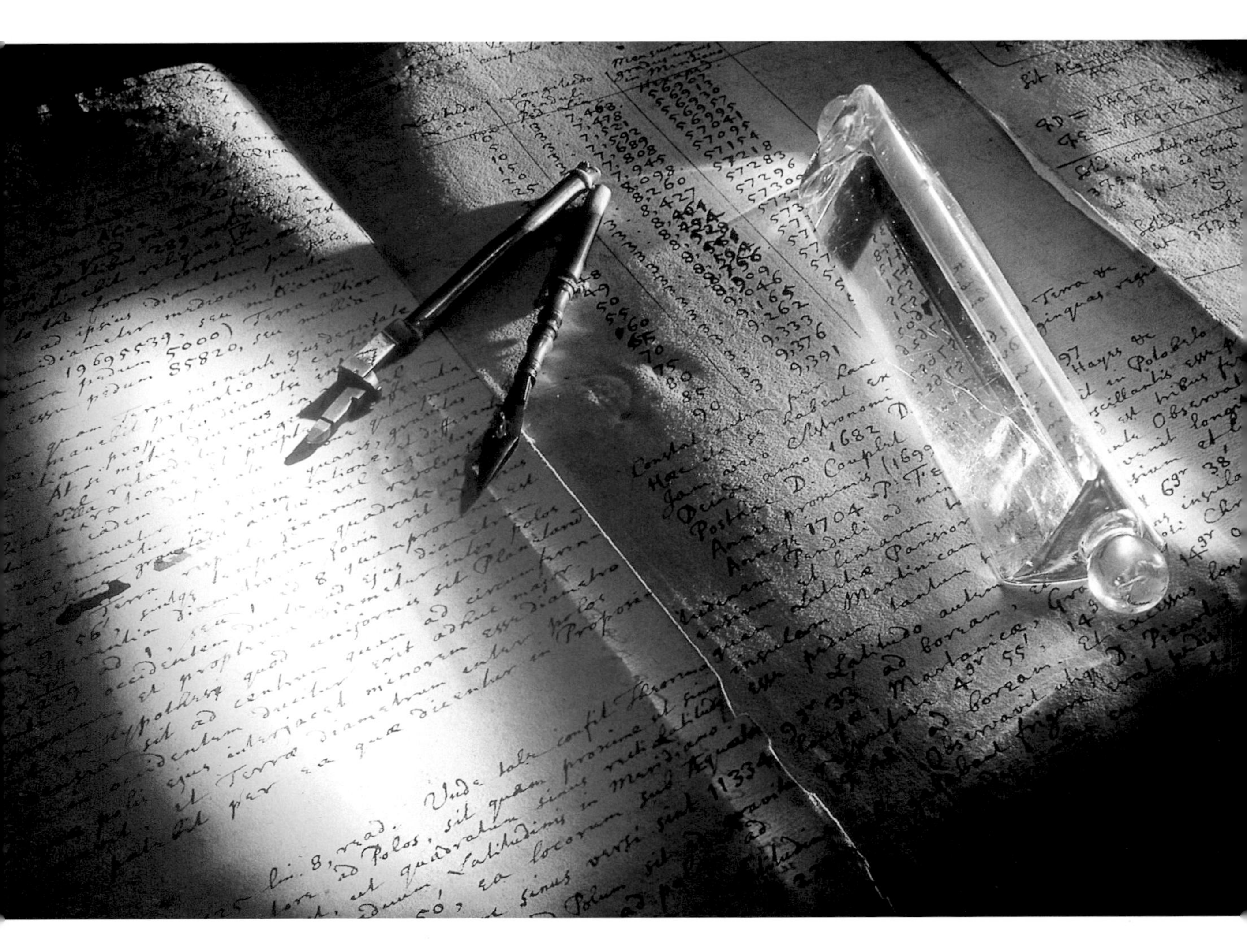

ABOVE: *One of the pages of Newton's book* Opticks. *A prism on top of the page splits light into separate colours.*

OPTICKS

Newton's second great book, called *Opticks*, was based largely on work he had done thirty years earlier, when he was a young undergraduate at Cambridge University. It was mainly about the behaviour of light, and explained refraction and reflection, rainbows, and the behaviour of mirrors and prisms. *Opticks* then discussed gravitation and the workings of the eye. The main parts of the book were arranged into three sections, each of which contained mathematical and experimental proofs of Newton's ideas.

Added to the end of *Opticks* were the 'Queries'. These were ideas that Newton couldn't prove, but which he suspected were true and worth investigating. Some of the 'Queries' formed the basis for quantum mechanics, a twentieth-century science that describes the behaviour of matter and energy. Other 'Queries' gave Einstein a starting point for his 'Theory of General Relativity', predicting that light from distant stars passing near the Sun would be bent by the Sun's gravity.

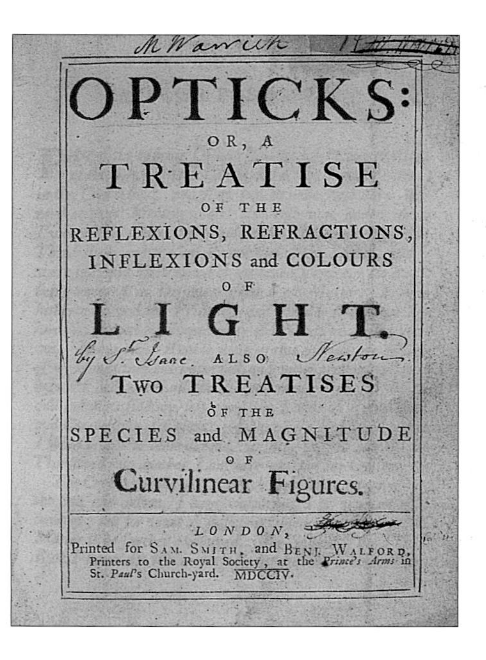

OPTICKS:
OR, A
TREATISE
OF THE
REFLEXIONS, REFRACTIONS,
INFLEXIONS and COLOURS
OF
LIGHT.
ALSO
Two TREATISES
OF THE
SPECIES and MAGNITUDE
OF
Curvilinear Figures.

LONDON,
Printed for SAM. SMITH, and BENJ. WALFORD,
Printers to the Royal Society, at the *Prince's Arms* in
St. *Paul's* Church-yard. MDCCIV.

ABOVE: *The title page of Newton's second great book,* Opticks.

Arise, Sir Isaac

In May 1705, Newton knelt before Queen Anne. She touched his shoulder with a sword and said, 'Arise, Sir Isaac.' Newton had been knighted. Strangely, it was not his brilliant scientific achievements that had earned him this honour so much as his political activities. Queen Anne was trying to draw the Whigs, including Newton, back into politics. Britain was at war with France, and Anne needed supporters to help her pay for the war. Giving a few knighthoods was a good way of getting that help.

IN THEIR OWN WORDS

'When I made [the telescope] an Artist in London undertook to [copy] it; but using another way of polishing [the mirrors] than I did, he fell much short of what I had attained.'

NEWTON DESCRIBING HIS INVENTION OF THE FIRST-EVER REFLECTING TELESCOPE, WHICH WAS OF AMAZING QUALITY, IN *OPTICKS*.

LEFT: *A painting of Queen Anne, who knighted Newton in 1705.*

IN THEIR OWN WORDS

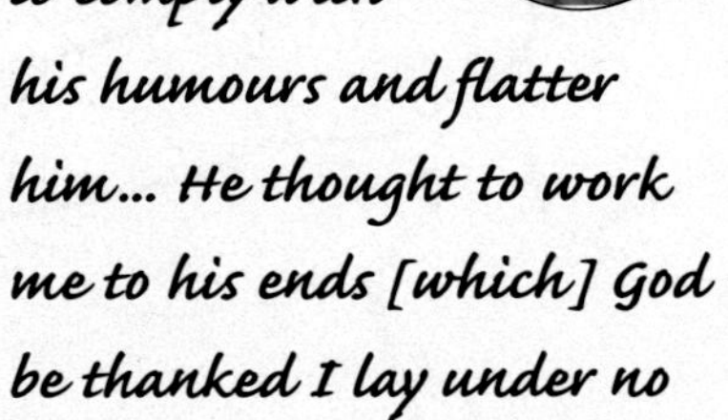

'His [plan] was to make me come under him, force me to comply with his humours and flatter him... He thought to work me to his ends [which] God be thanked I lay under no necessity of doing.'

JOHN FLAMSTEED ON ISAAC NEWTON IN 1719.

DISPUTES

Newton could not bear to be wrong or to have to explain himself, and he hated the thought that anybody but he could have come up with a brilliant idea. As a result he spent his last years locked in disputes with other scientists.

John Flamsteed

Between 1694 and 1696, Newton was embroiled in an argument with John Flamsteed, the Astronomer Royal. Newton's argument with Flamsteed centred around information about the movement of the Moon. Flamsteed had gathered this information from years of long nights crouched over a telescope, and was reluctant to give it to Newton until he knew what it was for. Newton needed the information for his new edition of *Principia*, and refused to explain himself. Between 1694 and 1696 the two men exchanged over forty-two letters, which slowly became less and less polite. By the 1700s, Newton had managed to wring most of the information he needed from Flamsteed, but their hatred of one another continued until Flamsteed's death in 1719.

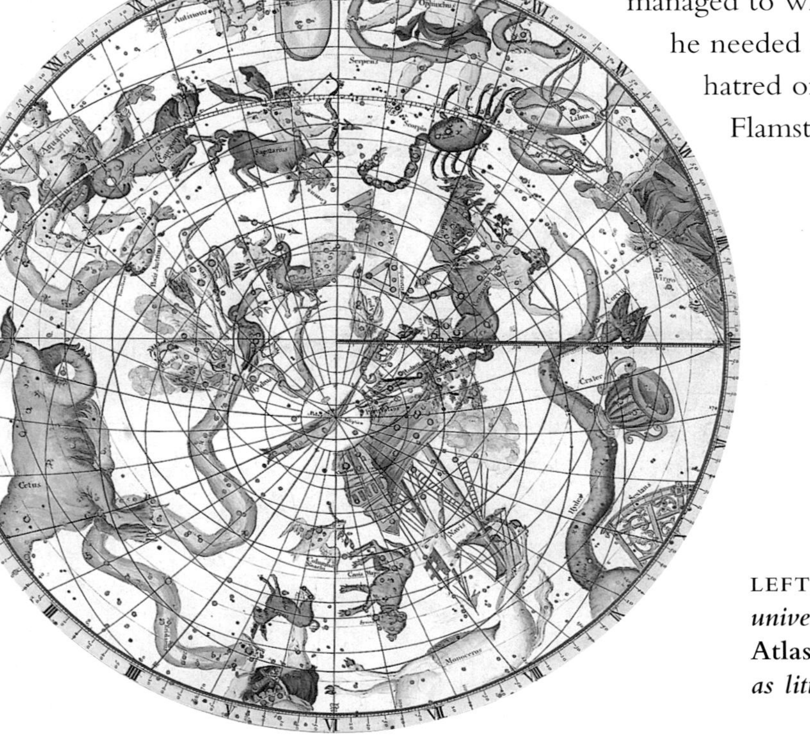

LEFT: *This is an illustration of the universe taken from Flamsteed's book* **Atlas Coelestis.** *The stars are shown as little gold dots.*

Gottfried von Liebnitz

Another dispute was with the German mathematician Gottfried von Liebnitz. In October 1684, Liebnitz published a paper on calculus. As soon as Newton heard about it he was furious. Before 1684, he and Liebnitz had exchanged letters, and in one of his letters Newton had referred to the calculus. He immediately assumed that Liebnitz had stolen his work, which at that time had not yet been published. Liebnitz, however, claimed that he had come up with his own version of calculus.

This wasn't good enough for Newton, who began a dispute that lasted for generations, as supporters of Newton and Liebnitz argued about it long after the two mathematicians had died. Like both Hooke and Flamsteed, Liebnitz found his name removed from the third edition of *Principia Mathematica*.

ABOVE: *Gottfried von Liebnitz (standing with his hand on the globe) at a demonstration in Berlin. Liebnitz was one of the most brilliant mathematicians of the 1600s, and had a long and bitter dispute with Newton.*

IN THEIR OWN WORDS

'[Newton] knew fluxions [a rate of change], but not the calculus of fluxions, which he put together at a later stage after my own was already published. Thus I have myself done him more than justice, and this is the price I pay for my kindness.'

GOTTFRIED VON LIEBNITZ, QUOTED IN *THE CORRESPONDENCE OF ISAAC NEWTON, VOL. 6.*

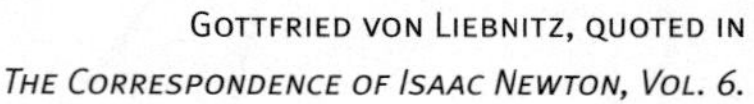

ABOVE: *Isaac Newton (behind the desk) chairs a meeting of the Royal Society in London.*

The Royal Society

Between 1703–27, Newton was President of the Royal Society. He used the Society to the advantage of himself and his friends, which almost always meant those who agreed with him, since Newton could not bear the idea that he might be wrong about anything.

Those who disagreed with Newton generally suffered as a result. Flamsteed had his name removed from the Society's records when he failed to pay his membership fees on time. Von Liebnitz suffered far worse: Newton formed a special committee to investigate the calculus dispute. The committee was packed with Newton's supporters, so it came as no surprise when they took his side in the argument, and declared that Newton had invented calculus first. Then the Royal Society, at Newton's urging, published their decision in a pamphlet that was distributed throughout Europe. Liebnitz, who was not wealthy, could do little in response except write letters.

In 1711, the Royal Society moved from its original home in Gresham College to new rooms Newton had chosen in Crane Court. It had been eight years since Robert Hooke had died. Somehow, all his instruments and his portrait were lost during the move. Newton had no reminders of his old enemy to bother him at the Society's new home.

However, there were good sides to Newton's character. He insisted on other members testing their ideas thoroughly, just as he did, and encouraged the talent of younger friends.

Newton also brought the Society's finances back from the brink of ruin. When he became President the society was badly in debt, but when he died it had plenty of money.

Final years

By 1723, Newton was in his eighties. By the standards of his day he was an extremely old man. Throughout the 1720s, Newton's health declined, but his stubbornness remained. When his doctors forbade him to walk, he refused, claiming that if he didn't use his legs, they would become even more useless. By 1727 Newton was seriously ill, and on 20 March, he died at his home in London.

RIGHT: *This portrait of Newton as a man of about forty-five years old belongs to the Royal Society. When he died, one of the world's greatest scientists was lost to the world.*

IN THEIR OWN WORDS

'[Newton has] the most fearful, cautious and suspicious Temper that I ever knew: And had he been alive when I wrote against his chronology [of the ancient kingdoms] I should not have thought it proper to publish... because I knew his Temper so well that I should have expected it would have killed him.'

WILLIAM WHISTON, WHO SUCCEEDED NEWTON AS PROFESSOR OF MATHEMATICS AT CAMBRIDGE, FROM *MEMOIRS*, 1749.

IN THEIR OWN WORDS

'Though his memory was much decayed, I found he perfectly understood his own writings, contrary to what I had heard.'

HENRY PEMBERTON, EDITOR OF THE THIRD EDITION OF *PRINCIPIA*, REMEMBERING A VISIT TO NEWTON IN 1722.

The Legacy of Newton

ISAAC NEWTON WAS BURIED in Westminster Abbey, London, on 4 April 1727. In 1731, his heirs erected a monument that still stands to one side of the Abbey, dominating an area known as Scientists' Corner. Nearby are buried Charles Darwin, who developed the theory of evolution, and many other famous British scientists.

Newton's discoveries about light and the movement of the planets are still relevant today. They were used to programme the first-ever flights to the Moon. But Newton's achievement is greater than this, because he was one of very few scientists who have changed the way we understand and think about the world. He did this by explaining how things work in a

LEFT: *Albert Einstein, whose Theory of Relativity was hinted at in some of the 'Queries' at the end of Newton's book* **Opticks.**

mechanical sense.

Imagine you own a car: you know that if you turn a key in the ignition, the car will start. If you put it into gear, the car will move. But can you explain how this happens? In the same way, people knew that the Sun rose in the morning and the stars moved at night, without understanding how. What Newton did – when no one else could – was to look at the planets and explain the mechanics of how they moved. In doing so he became one of the founders of modern science.

IN THEIR OWN WORDS

'Come celebrate with me in song the name Of Newton, to the Muses dear; for he Unlocked the hidden treasuries of Truth'.

FROM EDMOND HALLEY'S POEM *ODE TO NEWTON*.

BELOW: *In 1969, astronauts from the Apollo space programme became the first people to set foot on the Moon. Part of the science that helped put them there was developed 250 years earlier by Isaac Newton.*

Timeline

1543

Nicolas Copernicus publishes *De Revolutionibus* in Poland, raising the idea that the Earth travels round the Sun.

1564

15 FEBRUARY: Galileo Galilei is born in Pisa, Italy.
23 APRIL: William Shakespeare is born in England.

1600

Giordano Bruno is burned at the stake in Rome for claiming the Earth orbits the Sun.

1609

In Italy, Galileo begins making increasingly powerful telescopes and starts to observe the heavens. He becomes convinced that the Earth moves round the Sun. In Prague, now part of the Czech Republic, Johannes Kepler publishes *New Astronomy*, the first of two books containing his three laws of planetary motion (the second, *Harmony of the World*, was published in 1619).

1616

Edict from the Pope forbids Copernican theory.

1628

English physician William Harvey describes how blood circulates through the body.

1632

Galileo's *Dialogue* is published, supporting Copernican theory.

1633-34

Galileo is put on trial for heresy, for supporting the Copernican theory. His sentence is life imprisonment, though only a little of his time is spent in prison in Rome. Within eighteen months he is home again, but remains under house arrest until the end of his life

1638

Galileo's *Two New Sciences*, dealing with the new sciences of mechanics and motion, is published in The Netherlands.

1642

8 JANUARY: Galileo dies in Italy.
25 DECEMBER: Isaac Newton is born in England.
English Civil War begins.

1648

English Civil War ends.

1649

Charles I, King of England, is executed for treason.

1655

Newton goes to King's School, Grantham.

1658

Oliver Cromwell dies. Without Cromwell's powerful leadership, the Commonwealth government of Britain and Ireland begins to fall apart. Various groups start to argue with one another, paving the way for the return of Charles II.

1660

Charles II returns to England.

1661

Newton goes to Trinity College, at Cambridge University.

1665

Newton is awarded a degree. Outbreak of the plague in England. Newton returns to Woolsthorpe for two years to avoid the plague.

1666

1 SEPT: The Great Fire of London begins. A large part of the city is eventually destroyed. One good side-effect of the fire is that it kills many of the rats that had carried the plague in London. The plague dies down, and never returns as strongly again.

1667

Newton returns to Cambridge and is made a Fellow.

1669

Newton is made a professor of mathematics.

1675

'An Hypothesis Explaining the Properties Of Light' is read out to the Royal Society.

1679

Newton returns to Woolsthorpe to help nurse his mother through a fatal fever. She dies later that year.

1684

Edmond Halley asks Newton about proofs for the Inverse Square Law, following a bet made between himself, Christopher Wren and Robert Hooke in a London coffee shop.

1687

Principia Mathematica, Newton's book explaining the movement of the planets and comets through space, is published.

1689

Newton is elected to Parliament.

1696

Newton is appointed Warden of the Mint and moves to London.

1699

Newton is appointed Master of the Mint.

1703

Newton is elected President of the Royal Society.

1704

Publication of *Opticks*, Newton's book about the nature and behaviour of light.

1705

Newton is knighted by Queen Anne and becomes Sir Isaac Newton.

1727

Newton dies and is buried at Westminster Abbey, London.

1835

Galileo's *Dialogue*, which supported theories that Newton had proved correct by 1687, is finally taken off the Catholic Church's *Index of Banned Books*.

1905

Albert Einstein's 'Theory of Relativity', a development and mathematical proof of one of the 'Queries' raised in *Opticks*, is published. Einstein's work is crucial to our modern understanding of time and space, and made space travel possible.

Glossary

Alchemist
A person who aims to use complicated procedures to turn ordinary metals into gold.

Apothecary
A person who mixes together herbs, chemicals and other substances, to help people recover from illnesses or injuries. The modern equivalent of an apothecary's shop is a chemist's shop.

Catholic
Person who follows the Catholic branch of Christianity, which is led by the Pope in Rome.

Commonwealth
A Commonwealth is an independent state, usually a republic, or a community of states that join together. The Commonwealth of Oliver Cromwell was a government of Britain and Ireland that was led by Parliament rather than the king (who had been beheaded).

Counterfeit
Not real.

Element
A pure substance, which cannot be broken down into its component parts. Today there are over 100 recognized chemical elements. In Newton's day, the elements were earth, air, fire and water.

Elliptical
Shaped like a squashed circle.

Fellow
Fellows at Cambridge University were senior members, who were paid to carry on their studies and to do some teaching.

Holy Trinity
In the Christian religion, the Holy Trinity is made up of the God the Father, God the Son (Jesus) and God the Holy Ghost. These are thought to be the three forms of one God.

Mechanical
Newton and Galileo were among the first scientists to put their work on a mechanical basis. This means that they identified the system by which things were organized and then showed mathematical explanations for the system.

Orbit
The curved course of a planet or satellite around another body.

Parliament
A group of representatives of the people.

Parliamentarians
In the English Civil War, from 1642–46 and in 1648, the Parliamentarians thought that Parliament should rule England instead of the King.

Protestant
A branch of the Christian religion that does not accept the authority of the Pope in Rome.

Puritans
Members of a religious and social movement who wanted to reform the Church of England during the 1500s and 1600s.

Quarantine
Closing a place in order to stop the spread of disease.

Refraction
The process of turning or bending a ray of light when it passes at an angle from one medium to another of different densities.

Revelation
When God reveals knowledge that was previously hidden.

Royalists
Supporters of a king or royal government.

Tories
Members of a political party called the Tory party. Today's Conservative Party grew out of the old Tory Party.

Whigs
Members of a political party called the Whig party. Today's Liberal Democrat Party grew out of the old Whig Party.

Further Information

Further Reading

Super Scientists: Isaac Newton by Sarah Ridley (Franklin Watts, 2014)

Horribly Famous: Isaac Newton and his Falling Apple by Kjartan Poskitt (Scholastic, 2011)

Eureka: Isaac Newton and Gravity by Yoming S. Lin (PowerKids Press, 2011)

Graphic Discoveries: Isaac Newton and the Laws of Motion by Andrea Gianopoulos (Raintree, 2010)

Story Lives of Great Scientists by Franics Jameson Rowbotham (Benediction Classics, 2010)

Giants of Science: Isaac Newton by Kathleen Krull (Viking Children's Books, 2006)

Websites

www.isaacnewton.org.uk
Information about Newton's life, including a timeline, some extracts from Samuel Pepys's diaries and some quotes from Newton.

Isaac Newton Institute
www.newton.ac.uk
Cambridge University site containing information about Newton's life and works, including links to other Newton sites.

The Galileo Project, Rice University
http://galileo.rice.edu
Information on the life and work of Galileo, which also carries information about Newton.

Index

Page numbers in **bold** are pages where there is a photograph or an illustration.